Part of Leads Machines Series

LinkedIn

Leads Machines

Stop Wasting Time And Effort. Get This Blueprint To Generate Responsive Leads From LinkedIn Within 45 Days

KEITH CHOY

ISBN-13: 9781699333778

Text Copyright © Keith Choy

Legal & Disclaimer

The information contained in this book and its contents is not designed to replace or take the place of any form of medical or professional advice; and is not meant to replace the need for independent medical, financial, legal or other professional advice or services, as may be required. The content and information in this book have been provided for educational and entertainment purposes only.

The content and information contained in this book has been compiled from sources deemed reliable, and it is accurate to the best of the Author's knowledge, information and belief. However, the Author cannot guarantee its accuracy and validity and cannot be held liable for any errors and/or omissions. Further, changes are periodically made to this book as and when needed. Where appropriate and/or necessary, you must consult a professional (including but not limited to your doctor, attorney, financial advisor or such other professional advisor) before using any of the suggested remedies, techniques, or information in this book.

Upon using the contents and information contained in this book, you agree to hold harmless the Author from and against any damages, costs, and expenses, including any legal fees potentially resulting from the application of any of the information provided by this book. This disclaimer applies to any loss, damages or injury caused by the use and application, whether directly or indirectly, of any advice or information presented, whether for breach of contract, tort, negligence, personal injury, criminal intent, or under any other cause of action.

You agree to accept all risks of using the information presented inside this book.

You agree that by continuing to read this book, where appropriate and/or necessary, you shall consult a professional (including but not limited to your doctor, attorney, or financial advisor or such other advisor as needed) before using any of the suggested remedies, techniques, or information in this book.

CONTENTS

LinkedIn Leads Machines

INTRODUCTION

We all know how critical it is to have responsive leads for a successful business. With the rise of online spaces, getting leads through the Internet channels are getting easier than ever. And this is where this book comes in.

This book gives you a detailed blueprint on how to use LinkedIn to generate your own responsive leads. There will be 4 modules in this book with examples and checklists included at the relevant sections. The 4 modules are part of P.A.C.E blueprint which represent Profile, Attract, Content and Extract.

Module 1 – PROFILE: How to set up your profile with important settings and optimization strategies

When people do a search for you or your brand, they often go to Google. Your LinkedIn profile will most likely show up in the first three positions of the search results. It's often where those searching will click first to learn more about you. If your profile is slim or hasn't been updated since you first created it years ago, it may not be making the right first impression for prospective clients, customers, or potential partners. It's imperative to have an updated, optimized profile that quickly grabs attention and makes an impression. This module reveals the inner details and tips to optimize to raise your profile.

In this module, you will also get:

- Detailed checklist on how to set up your LinkedIn profile so that it's complete and optimized.

- Worksheet on all the necessary components to complete your profile so that you suck in the attention from your potential prospects

Module 2 – ATTRACT: How to optimize your LinkedIn Company page and profile to attract your leads in

You already know that LinkedIn is the social network aimed at building business connections and a place to assist you in your job-hunting endeavors. You probably already have a personal profile on LinkedIn. But do you have a LinkedIn company page set up and optimized for your business? If not, you should. It's easy to do. Once set up and optimized, you'll be available to a wider range of possibilities, from a large database of prospective employees to the use of an extended network to recruit new prospects.

In this module, you will also get:

- Detailed planning worksheet to help you generate content and headlines before uploading them to LinkedIn.

Module 3 – CONTENT: How to dominate with content on LinkedIn.

The content you share on LinkedIn builds your reputation. If it's quality, relevant information and entertaining, your reputation excels. If it's not relevant, is inconsistent and poorly constructed your reputation takes a hit. Like any part of an online business, keeping consistent with your content in social media can be difficult. It's hard to determine what to post, what type of content you should be using and what will get the most engagement for you. Learn here how to look at different styles of content and the best uses for each.

In this module, you will also get:

- Detailed checklist on what to share and how to create it consistently. This is key to dominating the content space.

Module 4 – EXTRACT: How to create a client outreach plan and extract out maximum prospect list

Reaching out via LinkedIn is the key to building your prospect list. But it should be done in a way that doesn't offend or annoy the prospect. And you don't want to reach out to everyone hoping that you connect with the right ones for you. In this book, you'll discover how to create an effective outreach funnel to build your prospect list.

In this module, you will also get:

- Detailed checklist to keep you on track as you start building relationships, you're your prospects.

- Detailed worksheet to help you as you begin reaching out and building relationships.

Let's start!

DOWNLOAD YOUR BONUS RESOURCES:

The following resources are available in our Bonus Online Resource Area at https://Linkedin.Leads-Machines.com/registration-bonus-membership

BONUS ONE
Checklists and Worksheets
All the 6 checklists/worksheets from our 4 modules so that you can print them out and fill in your details directly. This will save you effort and time.

BONUS TWO
Infographic on Getting New Leads
Infographic summarizing all the key steps you need to take. It is a good reference map which you will keep going back to.

BONUS THREE
LinkedIn Messaging Templates
These templates will help you optimize and build relationships with LinkedIn. No more writers' block. It includes:

- 2 Message Templates which you can personalize and use to get you started on getting recommendations on LinkedIn.

- 10 LinkedIn Prospect Messaging Templates to begin connecting with your LinkedIn prospects.

- 20 LinkedIn Headline Templates to help you come up with a killer headline. Your LinkedIn headline is one of the most visible areas on your profile. You want it to be intriguing, compelling, and interesting enough to get your prospects attention.

I BONUS FOUR
Relationship Building Tactics
Building relationships is key to getting leads to become customers. Use this list of 44 tactics as a guide.

BONUS FIVE
Strategies for LinkedIn Optimization Services mini-guide
As you already know, having a complete and fully optimized LinkedIn profile for any business is key to being seen among the millions on the social media platform. Many businesses just don't have the time or want to learn how to optimize their profile and Company pages. That's where your services come in. This mini-guide gives you a starting point on offering this much needed service.

Module One – PROFILE: Optimizing Your LinkedIn Settings and Profile

Is the first impression others see what you want them to know about your brand?

What message does your current LinkedIn profile make to potential clients?

Did you know your LinkedIn profile is almost as important as your website?

Do you know which sections of your profile are the most important?

Module One – PROFILE: Optimizing Your LinkedIn Settings and Profile

LinkedIn is one of the top social media sources for professionals to connect with others. According to LinkedIn, they are the "largest professional network with more than 610 million users in more than 200 countries and territories worldwide." With that many users it can be difficult to get eyes on your brand. That's why it's important your profile is optimized for maximum exposure.

When people do a search for you or your brand, they often go to Google. Your LinkedIn profile will most likely show up in the first three positions of the search results. It's often where those people searching will click first to learn more about you.

If your profile is slim or hasn't been updated since you first created it years ago, it may not be making the right first impression for prospective clients, customers, or potential partners. It's imperative to have an updated, optimized profile that quickly grabs attention and makes an impression.

The **first step is setting up your basic profile and optimizing in a way that grabs the attention of your target customers**. Specific settings will allow you to optimize your profile for maximum exposure.

Why optimize?

Your profile not only represents you and what you do, but your brand and company as well. Your LinkedIn profile needs to stand out from others. People do business with people they know, like and trust.

"To attract attractive people, you must be attractive.
To attract powerful people, you must be powerful.
To attract committed people, you must be committed.
Instead of going to work on them, you go to work on yourself.
If you become, you can attract."   *-- Jim Rohn*

With a generic profile, people are less likely to follow you and won't know if they can trust you. In fact, users with a complete optimized profile are 40 times more likely to receive opportunities from other LinkedIn users.

This book will dig into the strategies for creating highly optimized profile, why it's important to have an optimized profile, how to get recommendations, tips for creating headlines that get noticed and resources to help you boost your profile.

As you continue with the four modules in this book, you will learn how and why you should have a properly optimized profile (this module), the importance of a company page and how to optimize it, the tools, types, and tactics of posting content and finally, how to reach out to clients.

Let's get started.

Profile Optimization Strategies

Having an optimized LinkedIn profile simply means your profile is updated to get you the most visibility from your targeted audience. It involves several things including compelling, client-focused descriptions while establishing your credibility.

When you optimize your profile, it leaves an impression. The first seven seconds is all you get to wow when a potential client lands on your page. It's the difference between decision makers wanting to connect with you or them clicking away.

The advantages of having an optimized profile include:

- Attracting leads and clients
- Boost your professional reputation
- Create trust faster
- Build your authority
- Let's you stand out with a memorable impression
- Develop relationships with decision makers

Another advantage is your optimized LinkedIn profile will contribute to your digital selling efforts. Successful social selling and lead generation greatly depend on credibility and authority. Having a fully updated profile that is optimized is important to creating that credibility.

5 Best Strategies:

1. **Get found**. Make sure you are building your LinkedIn network with your ideal clients. Ensure you can be easily found on LinkedIn by the people you want to attract. Your network needs to be 1st, 2nd or 3rd degree connections or share a LinkedIn Group, otherwise you won't show up in their search results. Use the right keywords and search terms throughout your profile to be found by those searching for what you offer. Finally, make sure your profile is optimized and resonates with your ideal prospects.

2. **Tell your why**. Give your target audience a reason to look and listen to you. Your story is what separates you from your competitors. Tell them what your purpose is, what drives you, and why you do what you do. Then let them know how you can help them, what problem you solve with insights on how you solve specific problems.

3. **Create credibility**. Your profile needs to make you appear credible in the eyes of your potential clients. To do this, share recommendations from people who know you and have worked with you. The more recommendations you have that are detailed, the better you'll be able to establish trust.

   Having skills that are frequently endorsed by others is a great way to build trust. Your experience and achievements can also help. Toot your own horn, show off honors, awards, and recognition you've earned.

4. **Your ideal clients**. Make sure your summary highlights exactly who your ideal client is and what you can do for them.

5. **Call to Action (CTA)**. You must tell your readers what action to take. For example, create a CTA to download a free resource, schedule a consultation, send you an email or call you or whatever you want them to do next.

A complete profile should include:

- At least 5 skills
- A professional looking profile photo
- At least 50 connections
- Your industry and location
- A current position with description
- Two more past and current positions
- Education

Not only do you want your LinkedIn profile to be strategically optimized, you want it to be free of grammar and spelling errors. You must also ensure all the details are true and factual.

It doesn't matter whether you're wanting to attract potential business partners, recruiters, employees, or employers, or looking for new clients, having a truly complete LinkedIn profile only enhances your professionalism and your brand. It gives them reasons to connect and trust you.

Killer Settings For Maximum Exposure

An optimized LinkedIn profile is key to visibility. The first step is ensuring the basic information is correct. You need to let people know who you are first.

In this section I want to dig into the features / updates you need to be using to get the most out of presenting yourself and your business on LinkedIn for the best marketing view.

1. **Make a solid first impression with your name and headline**. Use your name without extra keywords. LinkedIn frowns on anything except your name in the name field. Instead, focus on using a keyword specific headline. The headline field, along with your name shows up in various places on LinkedIn.

   Create a snappy headline that's under 120 characters. Ensure it includes what you do in an original and creative way that's clear and informative.

   To edit the headline area, click on the Me icon on your LinkedIn home page. Select "View Profile". On your profile page, Click the pen or "edit" icon and put your content in the area for the headline. Click "Save" when you're done.

First Name *

Last Name *

Add former name

Headline *

Add variable keyword, compelling headline here

Add a high quality, professional headshot, 400 by 400 pixels, that is visible to everyone. Go to your profile and click on "Edit public profile and URL" found in the upper right corner. In the window that opens choose your visibility options. Choose "Public" to be visible through search engines and other networks.

Select a high-quality background cover image that portrays something about you. Make it one that is personalized or shows what you are about. You can create a background image easily on sites like canva.com. The correct size for the background images is 1584 by 396 pixels.

2. With recent updates, the contact information can now be seen at the top of your LinkedIn profile. **Update this with your website and blog URL, your Twitter** and other social media handles and your phone number or email address.

3. The **summary section on your profile** is where you enter a summary of your professional experience as well as your expertise. You are allowed several paragraphs to describe yourself to prospective connections such as employers, partners, customers, or clients. This is your elevator pitch.

You can add media to the top of your profile as well. Add the ones which you are particularly proud of to establish branding and your expertise.

You can use the following templates to help you fill out a complete summary that generates leads:

> WHAT I / WE DO:
> WHO I / WE WORK WITH:
> HOW I / WE DO IT:
> WHY IT WORKS:
> WHAT MAKES ME/US DIFFERENT:
> WHAT OTHERS SAY:
> AWARDS/PRESS
> READY TO TALK?

4. **Customize your LinkedIn URL to make it easy for others to find you**. Your unique URL is in the light-grey box below your name. Click the edit button to change it. A good custom URL would be www.linkedin.com/in/yourname.

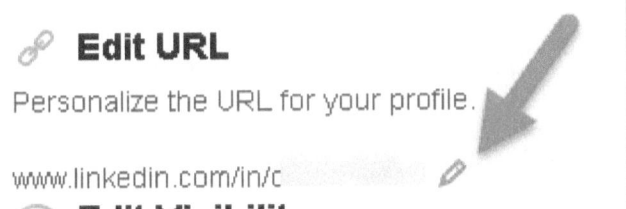

5. **Set your location and industry** to allow your profile to be displayed in searches of your field of expertise and your industry. Include a location and industry in your bio so anyone reading it knows what your focus is and where you are based.

6. **Include previous positions** so you audience can see you have experience and always deliver on your promises. Your previous history tells your story.

7. **Include recommendations**. Recommendations are like testimonials. These descriptive comments from former or current colleagues is persuasive content. Ask for them and give them freely to others.

Tips and Strategies

- Create a keyword-rich headline instead of leaving the default one provided by LinkedIn.

- Make your contact information easy to find in your profile and summary sections.

- Know who you're targeting before you build your content.

- Add the maximum of 50 skills and endorsements, putting your 3 most important skills first.

- Populate every part of the profile section that pertains to you with content to support your personal brand.

- Add a bit of personality to your brand story in the summary section.

- Include plenty of white space in your profile to make it easy to read.

- Use bullet points to highlight achievements, contributions, and awards.

Your profile is the first thing people will see when they come to your page. To stand out, it needs to be optimized completely.

Get That Recommendations

Your goal, once your profile is optimized, is to get recommendations from your connections for your work. Recommendations are essentially LinkedIn's version of testimonials which is attached to specific job experience in your profile.

Why You Need Recommendations

Social proof matters in our lives today. People use the internet to research products and services prior to purchasing. They read recommendations and reviews to help them make informed decisions before making a purchase or hiring services.

Recommendations show that someone trusted you to do the work and you did the job well enough that they were willing to write about you publicly.

The right recommendations are helpful in lead generation since they influence people to engage with you. People are more likely to trust products, services, brands, or individuals that several others have positively recommended.

LinkedIn recommendations are connected to individual profiles of real people. There cannot be a fake LinkedIn recommendation because you can follow it to the source of who wrote it and ask them questions about the person or service they recommended.

Correct Ways To Ask for Recommendations

It's best to ask for a variety of recommendations for specific skills or services you want to be known for. To achieve this, there are 2 channels. First you can use the "Request a recommendation" button for people you are connected with on LinkedIn. Second, you can email those whom you have worked with in the past (if you and your ex-colleagues aren't connected on LinkedIn).

To send an email asking for a LinkedIn recommendation, be courteous and professional and make it easy for them to say yes. Always offer to return the favor. Acknowledge they are busy and offer to write something they can edit. Give them an idea of what you are looking for within your recommendation, such as specific skills you used or the results you achieved for them.

To begin your request for recommendations, start from the person's profile you are making the request of. Click on the "More..." tab next to the blue message button at the top of their page, click on the "Request a recommendation." Fill out the form.

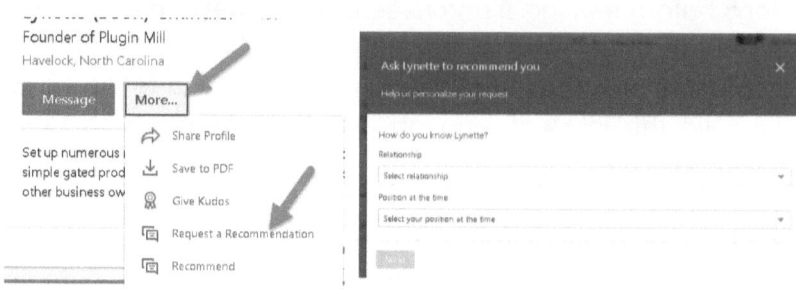

Be specific in your request. Don't use the default request for recommendation. Instead, write a sentence or two about the service you provided for them and the results and benefits they gained working with you.

Request a recommendation as soon as possible after completing a service while the results are still fresh in their mind. Be specific in what you want from them. LinkedIn will send you a notification that you have a recommendation you can accept to add to your profile.

LinkedIn recommendations are the testimonials that provide proof of others can trust you. They help others form opinions on you and how you can help them.

How To Get Your LinkedIn Headlines Noticed

Headlines are the 1 to 3 lines under your name. It's possibly the most important area of your LinkedIn profile.

So how do you write LinkedIn headlines that get noticed?

1. Start by searching other people in your industry on LinkedIn to find fresh examples of what their headline looks like. DO NOT COPY their headline.

2. Use your personality and think about how those you are targeting would think. What do you think they want to see? What words would they likely be searching for in a client, servicer, or provider?

3. Pluck a few sentences from your resume that best describe what you offer and condense them into a good headline sentence.

4. Always update your headline as you advance in your career and things change.

5. Use this formula to make your headline stand out:

   Job title/company plus Relevant Keywords plus Eye-catching statement about you/Something about you that makes others want to get to know you/personality

Your job title should, of course, be included as it shows relevancy to searchers. But you want to build your headline from here to make it stand out.

Use the right keywords and phrases that relate to your profession, your industry and describe you as a specialist. What terms or phrases do people use to search on LinkedIn to find you? Try to use several of those in your headline.

The final element in the equation is the eye-catching statement that will grab attention. It should be creative yet intriguing and memorable. Focus on how you do what you do. What makes your work special? What value do you offer? Use as many words as possible to make your LinkedIn headline standout.

There are several angles you can take when you write your headline. Below are some examples you can use:

- (Your role) helping (who) do (what). Begin with your job title and continue by explaining what types of companies you work with then what you do for them.

- List your area of focus or your credentials. List the type of work you do; awards you've received or your accomplishments. Separate them with commas, pipes, or bullets.

- If possible, combine both your focus and your credentials.

- Let your personality shine by telling a brief story about you, your work style or how you helped others.

Examples You Can Copy From

Here are three examples to help you think creatively:

Corporate Trainer (Kammy Haynes)
https://www.linkedin.com/in/kammyhaynes/

Travel Agent (Maria Stefanopoulos)
https://www.linkedin.com/in/mariastefanopoulos/

Maria Stefanopoulos · 2nd

⬤ Ingenious Travel ▦ Creating Unforgettable Group & Family Travel Experiences! ⬤

Tampa/St. Petersburg, Florida Area

LinkedIn Trainer (Trevor Turnbull)
http://linkedin.com/in/trevorturnbull

Trevor Turnbull · 2nd

Empowering Solopreneurs & Business Leaders To Transform Their B2B Sales Results | ExpertSellingMachine & LinkedIntoLeads

If you are having trouble coming up with a compelling headline, there are tools and templates available to help get you started.

The headline is one of the most important sections in your LinkedIn profile. Along with your image, it is what people see when they do a search. The best LinkedIn headlines are the ones that engage, surprise, or stand out in some way. Make sure yours does too.

Advanced Strategies To Boost Profile Views

So far, you've set up your basic profile and started doing a few tweaks to make it stand out. Now let's look at some more advanced strategies you can employ to boost views.

Use these tips to boost your views to your profile:

1. **Add media**. There are a variety of places you can add articles, videos, slideshows, images, and graphics to your profile. One place is the summary section. Another is place is under your individual job sections. Add links to your YouTube videos, SlideShare presentations or any other type of media.

2. **Cover image.** We talked a little about your cover image above. A cover image is optional but it's a great place to show off your branding. Create custom branding for yourself by creating a graphic that includes your branding or message. You can easily create a LinkedIn cover image using any graphics software such as canva.com.

3. **Keep in mind what your objective** is when you create your cover image. Is it to brand your company or industry?

Are you offering a benefit, appealing to a pain point or social proof? Do you want them to do something specific?

4. **Stay active.** LinkedIn prioritizes people who are active on its network. So it's important to increase your activity.

   a. Connect with others. On your My Network tab, look for recommendations for people you can connect with. Synchronize your email contacts to your LinkedIn account to find people you know.

   b. Join groups. In LinkedIn's search bar, type your interest(s) to find groups to join. On the results page, filter your results by groups. Request an invite to join. Be sure to add new posts and comments when you join.

   c. Post comments and updates. Share links to things you've read or seen. Post career lessons or tips. Comment on people's post in your network. Ask questions. Create updates automatically with tools like postcron.com.

   d. Write articles and share on the platform. Write entire blog posts on LinkedIn to boost your visibility. It's easy to publish by clicking on the "Write an article" button below your update box on your homepage.

5. **Be open for business.** Let others know you are actively looking for work. On your private dashboard, click on the section "Let recruiters know you're open" and turn this option to "on." You can write a note for recruiters; specify the type of work you're looking for and add locations on the next screen.

Even with the basic profile set up, you need to have a way to get yourself in from of potential partners or clients. Use these advanced strategies to optimize your profile to bring more views.

Great Resources Rolodex

Here is a list of online resources you can use to optimize your LinkedIn profile.

Headline creators

- Title-generator.com creates up to 700 headlines in one click.

- LinkedIn Headline Generator (https://www.linkedin-makeover.com/wp-content/uploads/linkedin_headline_generator/LinkedIn%20Headline%20Generator.html) can help you with your headlines.

Graphic and image resources

- Pixabay.com is a free image source.

- Canva.com is an easy to use graphic program that offers LinkedIn cover templates.

Content curation

- Pocket.com has a feature that allows you to curate content based on specific topics that is high-quality and credible.

- Feedly.com is simple and useful integrations. You can send content directly to Buffer or share it there then to your social profiles.

Here's What's Next

Your LinkedIn profile is the first thing people see when your page show up in their online searches. Therefore, it's important your profile is optimized fully so they get a good first impression.

In this module, you learned how and why you should optimize your profile along with tips to make it stand out. You learned what your settings should be for maximum exposure. You also went through the steps of adding a headline and your profile picture as well as setting up your summary and a customized LinkedIn URL.

You learned how to create a compelling headline and why adding a background image is important. Finally, you learned the strategies for getting more profile views.

The next step is to update your LinkedIn profile.

In the next module, you'll be learning why and how to create a LinkedIn business page and why it's important. You'll also get tips to optimize your page for best practices.

DOWNLOAD YOUR MODULE ONE RESOURCES:

Download the following resources for this module at https://Linkedin.Leads-Machines.com/registration-bonus-membership

RESOURCE ONE
Detailed checklist (3 pages) to help you set up your LinkedIn profile so that it's complete and optimized.

RESOURCE TWO
Worksheet (3 pages) to guide you to provide all the necessary components to complete your profile.

Module Two – ATTRACT: Optimizing Your LinkedIn Company Page/Profile

Module Two – ATTRACT: Optimizing Your LinkedIn Company Page/Profile

In the last module, you learned how to set up and optimize your LinkedIn Profile to so that your page can be found during online searches easier. This module will cover the importance of having a company page and the ways to optimize it.

You already know that LinkedIn is the social network aimed at building business connections and a place to assist you in your job-hunting endeavors. You probably already have a personal profile on LinkedIn. But do you have a LinkedIn company page set up and optimized for your business? **If not, you should.**

It's easy to do. Once set up and optimized, you'll be available to a wider range of possibilities, from a large database of prospective employees to the use of an extended network to recruit new prospects.

According to Hootsuite, LinkedIn has 562 million users and it's all about building your network and connections. It's about who you know and who your connections know.

Using LinkedIn for business, you can utilize your current connections to grow your brand and get new leads. Having an out-of-date personal profile will impact your leads and connections. If you want to grow your business and traffic, you need to have company page and profile.

According to LinkedIn, completed company pages often receive double the number of visitors as those with incomplete pages. And when your organization utilizes all the features and posts often you will generally gain followers up to six times faster than others.

In this module, you'll learn all the reasons why a LinkedIn company page and accompanied profile is important, how to set it up correctly, tips for optimizing it and hacks for getting more company profile views.

Don't Forgot Your Company Page

LinkedIn pages act as a hub page for your company. It's where people first meet you before they start doing business with you. It's a great way to establish your brand, share what you do and who your serve.

- Your LinkedIn company page boost your Search Engine rankings. When someone searches for your company name on Google, your LinkedIn company page usually comes up among the top 3 on the list. Creating a description that leads with powerful, keyword rich copy is essential because LinkedIn members search by keywords to find companies. For that reason, do include words and phrases that describe your expertise, your business and the industry focus you are in.

- The company page is a way to build your company brand by highlighting who you are and what you do for your company. It helps you attract and engage quality leads by sharing targeted content. You can feature videos, testimonials, and many other things relevant to your niche.

- Build your company credibility by having a LinkedIn company page. By adding your company name to your personal profile, you will be able to include your company logo and a hyperlinked link to the page. It gives a more professional appearance.

- LinkedIn company pages are an excellent way to take advantage of the network effect of your market, friends of your friends or acquaintances who knows someone. Visitors will see mutual connections and may be more likely to choose your business over your competitor.

- With a LinkedIn company page, you can share press releases and blog posts and connect with other businesses while attracting followers.

After optimizing your LinkedIn profile, adding a company page is the next step in growing and getting seen by future clients and leads.

4 Key Steps To Setup Your Page

LinkedIn is the perfect place to drive business results while raising brand awareness and educating your potential customers on what you sell. Using rich content and compelling post updates helps you establish yourself as a brand leader in your niche.

Now that you know why you should have a LinkedIn company page for your business, let's get busy setting up your page. If you don't already have a personal LinkedIn profile, you'll need to set that up first.

Step 1: Add your company

Go to the LinkedIn Marketing Solutions portal at https://business.linkedin.com/marketing-solutions/linkedin-pages to begin creating your company pages.

Click on the "Create a Company Page" button.

Then choose the type of business you have. This is self-explanatory, but be aware that showcase pages are for specific areas of your company such as a page to represent a brand, business unit, organization initiative, etc. It is not meant for short-term marketing campaigns.

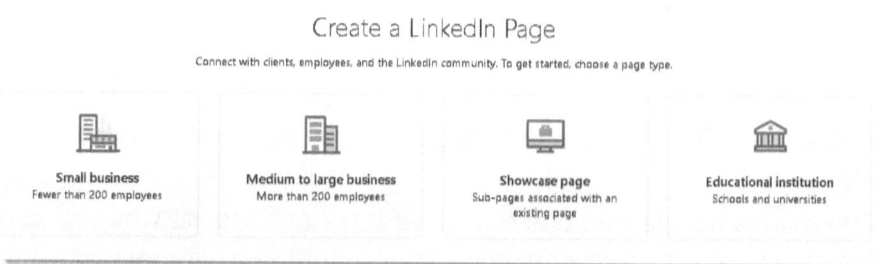

Step 2: Add Page Details

Enter your name or company name, the URL for people to find your business on LinkedIn and your website in the Page Identity section.

In the Company details section, choose your industry, your company size, and the type of company you have.

In Profile details is where you can upload your logo. The recommended size is 300 by 300 pixels. Your company logo is used instead of a profile picture that is normally found on social networks.

Add your tagline in this section as well. It doesn't have to be your final one as it can be changed later.

When you're done, tick the "I verify that I am the official representative of this company and have the right to act on behalf of the company in the creation of this page."

Finally, click the blue "Create page" button.

Step 3: Admin Page

On the next screen you will be taken to the admin page where you can see your updates, dashboard, add a cover photo and make any changes.

Click on the edit pen to add a cover photo that represents your company. It should be 1536 by 768 pixels.

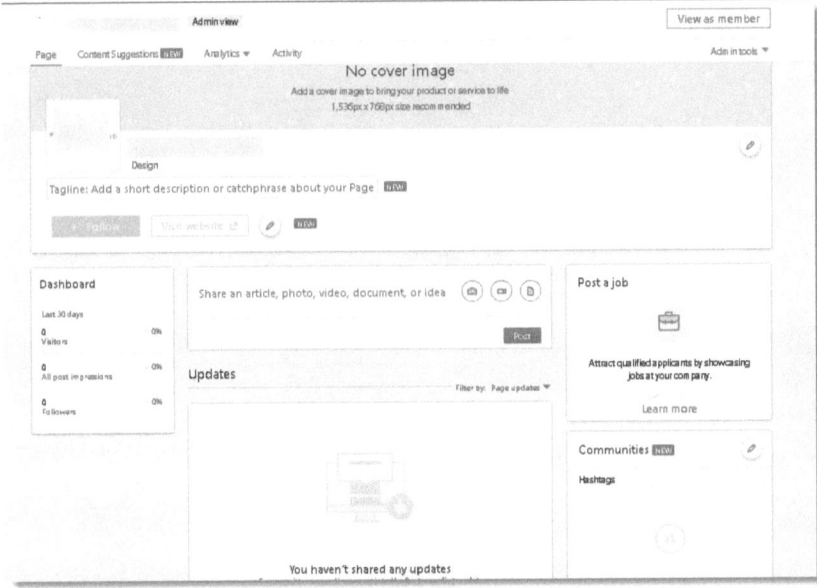

In the About section, describe what your company does and why potential customers should follow you. You have up to 2000 characters to get your marketing message out. Add up to 20 company specialties. These are like the keywords or tags that people use to find your business on LinkedIn. You should also include your various products, services, and strengths here.

In this section you will need to provide at least one location for your business as well.

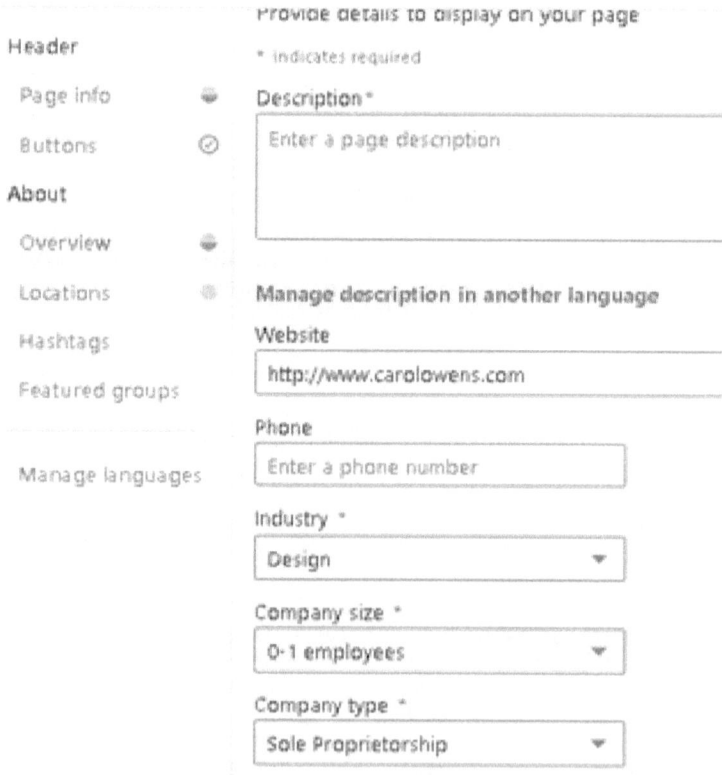

Step 4: Publish your page

When you are ready, click Publish button for your company page to go live. You can preview your page by clicking on the member view tab at the top far right of the page. If you don't like what you see, click "Manage page" to make any changes.

Your page is set up. But you're not finished yet. Your page needs to be optimized so it can be found.

5 Best Practices to Optimize to Get That Lead

According to LinkedIn, **companies with complete information get 30% more weekly views**. Therefore, you need to have complete and accurate information in your profiles.

There are several areas that should be completely and strategically filled out on your company page. Let's look at each of them.

Branding Creatives

Promote your brand recognition by adding the creatives that make up your brand. On your LinkedIn Company page, you need a company logo in the size of 300 x 300 pixels. Use your logo instead of a picture of your team or yourself here.

A cover image sized 1536 X 768 should be used instead of the generic LinkedIn image. The cover photo can be a clean, clear image of your products, a promotional banner for one of your services or an area to advertise that you're hiring or participating in a special event. Whatever you choose, make it exclusive to LinkedIn to make your profile unique.

Here are two examples of a well thought out cover image with logo.

About You

Completely fill in the About You section on your LinkedIn company page. This section is a glimpse into the highlights of what your company does. It's directly beneath the overview tab so it needs to be fully optimized with a solid description telling your potential leads what makes your company unique and what your motto or vision is. It can talk about what products or services you offer as well. Try to include long-tail keywords in the description.

In this section, includes in details to these six questions:

- Who are you?
- Where are you based?
- What do you offer?
- What are your values?
- What is your brand voice?

- How can people reach you to learn more?

In the Company details section include all the things that make your business special or stand out from a crowd can be included in the specialties section.

Life Tab

The Life tab helps you give a picture of your company's culture. It allows you to promote your work environment, show off your employees, present the impact you make on the local community and any other way you want to showcase your business.

Not only can you add text and graphics to the life tab, but you can integrate multiple videos as well.

Showcase Pages

This is the section to add additional products, services or other brands or units associated with your main company. For each product, service, or additional business, you can create showcase page. These independent pages have their own About Us section, its own followers, post updates and independent analytics.

For example, if your main business is XYZ Consulting but you also offer web design services under XYZ Web, you can have a Showcase page for that.

Consistent postings

The visual and basic settings are important for optimizing your company profile page. But it's important to post quality content on a consistent basis to keep your audience growing and returning.

You should aim to post at least one update a day. Share blog posts you've written, posts or articles from other websites relevant to your industry, ask questions of your audience or some other pertinent content.

Keep in mind, the LinkedIn audience is different from other social networks. It's less about sales and marketing and more about highlighting your industry expertise, employees, job opportunities and content relevant to your industry.

Strategically optimizing your Company profile page is a key factor in building your following on LinkedIn. Completely fill out all the sections using targeted keywords and descriptions, having your visuals match your brand and creating consistent content. Next, we'll discover some unusual hacks to get more company page profile views.

9 Hacks To Pull In More Views

Now that your company page profile is filled out and strategically optimized, you want to implement the following 9 little known hacks to get more views to your page.

1. Use LinkedIn Groups to find more customers, learn about your audience and network with other in your industry. You can follow others, start conversations, or engage in relevant conversations.

2. Don't be shy about asking for as many endorsements as you can (note: more than 99 can be seen on your profile). More than a billion peer-to-peer endorsements have already been given on LinkedIn. It's a powerful and sometimes controversial form of social proof of your trustworthiness. And it's mutually beneficial to both you and your contact giving the endorsement.

3. Involve your employees in your Company page. Allowing your employees to post company related content using a platform like Bambu, is one of the best ways to grow your LinkedIn presence and drastically increase your content's reach

4. Create a clickable profile badge and add it to your email signature, your blog and everywhere it can be clicked on.

5. Make your video content priority. Education videos to company commercials to company product how-to, people are being entertaining and craving videos over written content.

6. Consistency is key in building your network. Come up with a consistent content calendar specific to LinkedIn. And know the best times to post on LinkedIn for engagement. Post at least once a day.

7. Know and understand your analytics. Your audience insights and which of your posts are the top performers. This helps you create more of the same type of content and personalize it to your audience.

8. The first 6 words on mobile device or 2 lines from a desktop in your summary show in an initial search so make sure your company summary stands out in those few words/lines.

9. Remove pending connection requests if you've sent a connection request and they haven't responded. Do so by going to My Network, click on manage all and then click on sent tab.

Try these little-known company page hacks to increase your views and begin building a wider network.

What's Next

So far, you've learned why you need an optimized LinkedIn profile and how to set it up. Then you learned how to optimize your LinkedIn Company page and profile and the best ways to strategically optimize it for the most views.

Just like any networking you do, setting up a LinkedIn page is important for your company's growth. It allows you to be seen in a professional way while building your credibility, boosting your reach, and highlighting who you are.

Setting up your LinkedIn Company page takes a few steps, but, when done correctly, doubles your reach. Adding a company banner and logo, filling out a compelling summary and highlighting your best products or services will help in optimizing your page.

Strategically setting up your page, consistently posting to the page and connecting to more contacts will bring in more views. This allows you to build and grow your current and future network quickly.

In the next module, we'll learn how to dominate our LinkedIn content. We'll discuss the different types of tools, content, and tactics to post regularly on LinkedIn.

DOWNLOAD YOUR MODULE TWO RESOURCES:

Download the following resources for this module at
https://Linkedin.Leads-Machines.com/registration-bonus-
membership

RESOURCE ONE
Detailed planning worksheet (3 pages) to help you generate
content and headlines before uploading them to LinkedIn.

Module Three – CONTENT: Dominating Your LinkedIn Content

Module Three – CONTENT: Dominating Your LinkedIn Content

In the last module, we discussed the importance of having a company page. You learned the best strategies for optimizing it and how to get more views to it. This week you'll learn how to dominate your LinkedIn content. This book discusses the tools, types, and tactics to be using to post content regularly on LinkedIn.

The content you share on LinkedIn builds your reputation. If it's quality, relevant information and entertaining, your reputation excels. **If it's not relevant, is inconsistent and poorly constructed your reputation takes a hit.**

Like any part of an online business, keeping up with consistent content in social media can be difficult. It's hard to determine what to post, what type of content you should be using and what will get the most engagement for you.

In this module, we're going to look at different styles of content and the best uses for each. For example, should you be posting videos of your employees or videos of products? Are SlideShare presentations allowed on LinkedIn? What is Pulse and how do you use it?

Then we'll look at choosing the right content. You'll also learn what types of content you shouldn't post on LinkedIn. Finally, we'll share tips on how to use content curation, Private Label Rights (PLR) content, and other rebranded content to make it easier to stay consistent.

Let's get started.

6 Must-Know Types of Content

The content you share on LinkedIn doesn't have to solely written posts. Instead think of all the ways you share content on your website, other social media accounts and within your company. You want to use content that will be the most engaging to your audience and distribute your brand message across the platform.

Here are the main types of content recommended on LinkedIn and their different uses:

Videos - Videos are one of the easiest ways to grab attention. You can share stand-out content that others will find compelling by sharing your professional tips or demo, lectures, and conversations. Record and share an explainer video. Use video to engage viewers by asking a question. Video is also great for sharing everyday work moments to give LinkedIn network a backend view.

Post with a video

Best tips:

- Hook viewers quickly by having a striking visual or thought-provoking opening line.

- Show your followers what you see.

- Keep the length around 30 seconds to two minutes long.

- Film in a quiet spot if possible, Otherwise, use your headphones or an external microphone for clear sound.

- Create quality videos with a clear picture and good lighting. Film vertically for the best view.

- Use the right #hashtag to get your content discovered.

Images - Images are one of the most effective types of content. Images help you stand out by attracting like-minded customers who relate to your brand. Images can be used in both posts and articles. Images can be easily repurposed in other content.

Post with an image

The types of images you can present are unlimited. Examples includes:

- Lifestyle featuring your product or service
- Events
- Company atmosphere and culture
- Cartoons
- Memes
- Gifs
- Behind the scenes images
- Product creation images

Best tips:

- Tell a story of your brand.

- Use clear high-quality images

- Use strong keywords behind your image alt tags

- Use images that people can relate to or that evoke emotion.

SlideShare - SlideShare is LinkedIn's hub for professional content including presentations, infographics, and other types of documents. Sharing slides can help you build your reputation while encouraging more opportunities to grow.

To access the SlideShare screen, click on the "work" tab arrow (referring to the diagram below), then click on the "SlideShare" button.

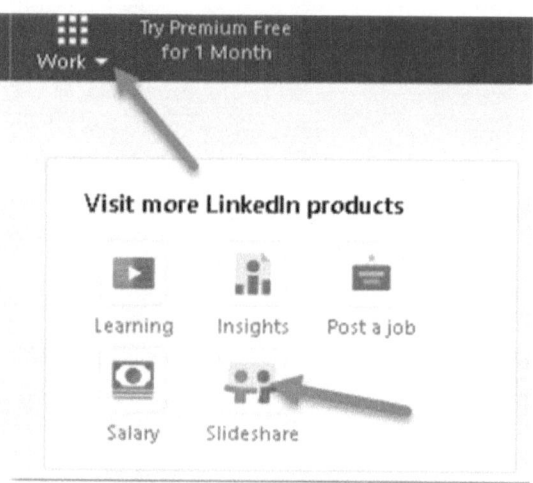

Best tips:

- Use the fundamentals of good design: Balance, Emphasis, Unity and Movement on your presentation.

- **Draw your viewers eye to upper third or lower third**

- Choose text-friendly images and photos

- Use images that people can relate to or that evoke emotion and support your theme

- Use typography as emphasis to text or support a certain style

Posts - Posts are short, quick bursts of text to stay connected to your community. Sharing posts on LinkedIn sparks engagement, increase your brand reach, and build your relationships. These posts are also broadcasted to the LinkedIn feeds of your connections' homepage. The text limit for posting is 1300 characters which is about five lines. Anyone can post an update on their LinkedIn page.

Best Tips:

- Share consistently to build relationships around your content

- Use relevant hashtags to help your content get discovered

- Share quality insights and fresh perspectives on trending topics

- Join other conversations and engage your own network by asking questions

- Invite people into your conversations by @mentioning them in the post.

- Use images and other rich media such as videos to draw people in and add life to your post.

Pulse - Pulse is LinkedIn's publishing platform. This is mainly the place for publishing full length articles to share your knowledge and expertise. It can include links, videos, and images as well. You can write in-depth about your challenges, opportunities, professional expertise, trends happening in your industry and anything relevant to your company. There is no limit on the length of the article.

Best tips:

- Longer articles get the best reception- around 500-1,000 words
- Use compelling headlines that prompt readers to click through
- Use cover photos to get more engagement
- Use relevant keywords within your article
- Have publishing schedule and publish fresh content frequently
- Cross-promote your content on your other social sites
- Publish at times when business professionals are most likely to check their feed

When trying to decide what content or article to write, ask yourself these questions:

- What will or should your industry look like in 5, 10 or 15 years? How will it get there?
- What are some important trends people in your industry know?
- What challenges have you faced or opportunities have you seized?
- What is the biggest problem that needs solving in your industry, in your opinion?

- What advice would you give someone just entering your field?

- What skill is essential in your job? Why

- How has your industry or profession changed since you began?

- How did you get started in your industry, profession, career?

- What advice do you have for advancement in your profession?

- What would you do or do differently if you started all over and why?

Sponsored Content - If you have a LinkedIn company page, you can take your most valuable content and turn it into sponsored content. This content reaches the people most likely to need your information.

Best Tips:

- Use genuinely valuable content like an ebook, guide, how-to or template

- Add visually inviting images, thumbnail size

- Use a captivating headline that answers the "What's in it for me?" question from your prospect

- Take advantage of curated content as it might have a higher click-through potential

The types of content you can use on your LinkedIn Business/profile are varied. You want to post a variety of content consistently to stay in front of your audience. You can do this by creating a content schedule and plan incorporating images, posts, articles, videos and SlideShare presentations.

Best Ways To Using PLR Content

Consistently producing content is necessary for growth. But creating all that content can be exhausting. To post content continuously without being overwhelm, you can use private label rights (PLR) products and other types of rebranded content.

Private label rights products are prewritten content that is sold with the rights for you to use as your own content. By adding to, changing to fit your niche, and personalizing it, PLR is a quick way to add content to your LinkedIn account. Many PLR providers provide articles, videos, and other types of content in their packages that can easily be posted.

You can use PLR products to create articles on LinkedIn, videos, or quick post updates. Use the PLR to create SlideShare presentations, social media graphics or any other type of content.

If your business has a blog (and it should), you can republish your posts on your LinkedIn profile or as an article in Pulse. Once your article is published on your website, wait a day or two and then republish it on LinkedIn.

Use the "Write an article" button in LinkedIn to begin a new article. Add your image at the top of the article. You can use a different image or the same one from your original post. Paste in your content from your blog post. Tweak the headline so that it's different from the original post.

Make any changes to the content such as highlighting the important points. You don't want an exact copy of the original post. You want to expose your message to a wider audience. Include a call to action in your article and link back to the original post.

Another option for your blog post is to share snippets or quotes from the post and publish as a post update on LinkedIn

You can repurpose content from its original form into another form to share on LinkedIn.

- Turn your webinar into a video tutorial
- Turn a video tutorial into an article
- Turn your webinar slides into LinkedIn graphics
- Update old blog posts with new content you share on LinkedIn
- Turn a PowerPoint Presentation into a SlideShare presentation
- Share Interviews as case studies
- Turn your visual content into inspirational graphics to share on LinkedIn
- Convert your Q & A / FAQ into an infographic to share on LinkedIn
- Turn an infographic into a SlideShare presentation
- Transcribe a podcast episode into an article to share on Pulse

Content repurposing and using Private Label Content allows you to get many uses from a single piece of work without having to completely create something new. The research and work have already been done, it's just a matter of putting it into a new format.

4 Ways To Creating Engaging Content That Will Pass LinkedIn Feed Spam Filter

Providing content that engages your audience is key to building your network. Engagement is one of the main goals of social media marketing. In fact, according to <u>LinkedIn Marketing Solutions</u>, 50% of LinkedIn members will buy from companies they have engaged with.

Content plays an important role in attracting your audience. Creating engaging content is key to keeping them. You can do this in many ways.

1. **Tell a story**. Storytelling can and should be a part of every piece of content you produce. You can incorporate how you came to the solution, your process along the way or some story that leads well with the article.

2. **Use awe-inspiring images or images that tell a story**. Don't just show your product on a plain white background. Instead show images of customers using your product.

3. **Create compelling headlines and engaging first sentences**. The first line should grip your attention: interesting, unusual, emotional, shocking are all human emotional needs that grab out attention.

4. **Personalize it**. Even though LinkedIn is where B2B professionals hang out, people still want to do business with real people. Let your personality and your brand's personality come through in all your content.

It helps to understand how the LinkedIn algorithm works as well when creating engaging content. It's designed to make your homepage feeds inviting. The LinkedIn feed has a spam filter that determines whether your content will show in the feed, how far an audience it reaches or if you are a spam user.

Here is how the algorithm works:

> **Stage 1:** A computerized bot evaluates your content as spam, low-quality or clear. You want to have clear content to move to the next stage.
>
> **Stage 2:** The algorithm then measures the initial user engagement such as likes, comments and shares. This signals that your content is good enough to move to the next stage. If you are flagged for some reason as spam by users or hide it from their feeds, LinkedIn's algorithm believes it as negative content. Make sure your content is relevant to other's professional lives. Is it offensive? Are you over-posting? Is your post unique and insightful?
>
> **Stage 3:** The algorithm further checks for spam and credibility and quality based on your account and network to determine if the content is spam. The algorithm determines the usefulness and relevance of the post. Engagement is very important at this stage.
>
> **Stage 4:** In this stage, human editors review the content. They determine whether it should be displayed, boosted, or demoted.

Create engaging content that passes the LinkedIn algorithm is necessary for people to see your updates. Learning how LinkedIn's algorithm works helps you create content that will be seen over and over.

Content Curation and Automation

Now that you know why you need to create engaging content and the algorithm for LinkedIn, it's time to learn about ways to automate your content creation. Content curation and automation tools make being consistent easier. There are many types of content that can be used for all your content needs.

Content curation is gathering a collection of content and adding value and your voice to it. The content comes from a variety of sources, around a specific topic which you share with your followers. You sift through articles on the internet, collect those that are the most interesting and relevant to your industry and share them in blog posts and on LinkedIn.

Content curation allows you to create posts quickly using other people's content the right way. You're sharing resources and rare content that isn't the same article found on a million other feeds.

Benefits of Content Curation:

- Saves you time and energy
- Elevates your brand visibility
- Establishes your authority and thought leadership

Best Tips for Curating Content

- Instead of automatically posting regurgitated content, add meaning and value that is relevant to your potential customers. Add detailed comments, comparisons, and your opinion on the subject or just a short blurb to summarize the content.

- Monitor trends and curate content that is current as well as evergreen content.

- Ask your viewers what they are interested in.

- Mix your content with curated content to make it promotional as well as educational.

- Include your user-generated content.

- Share your personal observations about developments that have happened over the past 5 to 10 years in your industry.

- Give your audience what it wants. Research what they are sharing, what information they are seeking or the latest industry trends they are following. Are they looking to be entertained or inspired?

- Source only valuable content using automated tools.

- Make it look good. Don't just throw a bunch of content together. Make it flow and consistent with your brand style.

- Always be ethical and credit the creator of the work.

Next you want to automate as much as you can to keep content consistently in your LinkedIn feed. Use a social media calendar to determine what you're going to post. Then use tools and programs to schedule your posts. This way the work is done once and then can be posted hands off.

Automation tools are great for scheduling any batch writing you do as well. By creating and scheduling posts in bulk, you free up time that can be used in better ways.

Suggested Automation Tools To Fire Up Your Effort

Use one of these suggested programs:

1. Hootsuite (https://hootsuite.com/platform/content-curation) offers a bulk composer feature to make it easy to schedule post across different social networks at once, including LinkedIn.

2. Pocket (https://getpocket.com/) is an app that lets you gather content in one place from your browser or from apps like Pulse.

3. Feedly (https://feedly.com/i/welcome) is the most popular RSS and blog reader online. It allows you to subscribe to your favorite websites, blogs, publications, and YouTube channels, getting the content to read, save or share it.

4. DrumUp (https://drumup.io/) is an app that goes through tons of web content to bring you the freshest and most relevant stories.

5. Shareist (https://www.shareist.com/) allows you to research and capture, collaborate and create content, plan your sharing strategy, and share the content on social media.

6. Buzzsumo (https://buzzsumo.com/) is packed with helpful features. You can search for the most shared content using keywords, domains, or specific types of content like guest post or videos.

7. Quuu (https://quuu.co/) offers a free plan. This content curation program is the only tool where each and every piece is hand-reviewed by humans. Quuu sends the content directly to your Hubspot or Buffer schedule.

8. Curationsoft (http://curationsoft.com/) is a desktop-based curation software that allows you to find, evaluate and curate content into a drag and drop HTML editor. It can be used to create a blog post that you share on LinkedIn or used as an article on LinkedIn.

Content curation is a time and money saver every business should be incorporating in their marketing strategy. Using one of the many tools available to curate the content for you makes it even easier to share quickly.

16 Types of Content You Can Start Today

Now that you know why you need to curate content and how to do it easily, you might be wondering what types of content to post. The type of content can be anything, well, almost anything.

It can be things like ...

1. **Everyday stuff** (related to the business and not related) This can be as simple as what or where you had dinner with your amazing team or the fishing trip you made with your family. Take on a spicy (and tactful) point of view on a trending non-business topic

2. **Industry information.** LinkedIn is a business to business platform so it's only logical to share content related to your industry. You can share reports, whitepapers, long-form content, videos.

3. **Post Results**. Did your company participate in a competition recently? Post the results of how you did. Post results of how a new marketing campaign or product launch fared.

4. **Case Studies**. Show your audience how others have used your product and services through a case study.

5. **Share articles you like**. Don't just talk about you and your company. Share articles from your competitors and others in your industry that are trending and interesting.

6. **Post industry statistics**. People love statistics so share industry and company stats as part of your marketing campaign.

7. **Share client testimonials**. Gather testimonials and endorsements from your satisfied clients to boost your authority and leadership.

8. **Share how to videos and articles**. Share videos along with articles on how to use your products or services for the best results. Use list-style posts as well. Marketing guru Neil Patel has built a following using this style of posts on LinkedIn.

9. **Product launches and feature updates**. Keep your audience aware of the latest products or services you have.

10. **Offer quick tips**. These simple and short posts include leadership tips and tricks that encourage productivity, leadership, and professional success. Or offer simple text quotes relevant to your followers.

11. **Share company updates**. Find interesting and visual ways to share company updates on what's happening in your company. It's a great way for your audience to get to know you and your company better.

12. **Share photos** of your company, your employees, and the activities they do daily. Share photos taken at business events you attend.

13. **Humanize your company**. Highlight your best employees as thought leaders.

14. **Use Showcase pages** to drive registration to events your company is hosting or sponsoring.

15. **Share lessons learned**. It doesn't matter what your age or industry is, you have learned important lessons that others can benefit from. Share them with others.

16. **Make predictions**. It doesn't matter whether you are right or wrong, predictions are a way to get a discussion going.

What Happens Next

Content is the key to building your following on LinkedIn. You want to dominate with your content through consistency, quality, and variety. To do this you need to use tools for automating the process, use other people's content correctly and post a variety of types of content.

The styles of content you use depends on your topic as much as how you want to present it. A video might be the right fit for certain topics while a SlideShare presentation would fit better for others. Sometimes a quick funny image is all you need to share.

Whichever style of content you choose, the key is making it quality and relevant. One way to do that is to curate content about your industry. Curated content can save you time and money. And with automation tools you can put together a curated piece in a fraction of the time of doing it yourself.

The type of content you present is as wide as you want it. Post updates on your company or products, show research you've done, or share videos about your employees or brand. Keep your followers up-to-date on what's happening in your business, the industry, and upcoming trends. Finally, humanize your brand by posting about non-business events occasionally.

In the next and final module, you will learn the proper way to reach out to prospects on LinkedIn and how to introduce yourself and your business. Reaching out to prospects is necessary for building relationships and getting more business.

DOWNLOAD YOUR MODULE THREE RESOURCES:

Download the following resources for this module at
https://Linkedin.Leads-Machines.com/registration-bonus-membership

RESOURCE ONE
Checklist (4 pages) to help you learn what to share and how to create it consistently.

Module Four – EXTRACT: Capturing Your LinkedIn Leads

Module Four – EXTRACT: Capturing Your LinkedIn Leads

In the previous module, we discussed how to dominate your LinkedIn content through the styles and types of content you use. And you learned how to use content curation to make posting consistently easier. This time we'll be talking about the proper way to reach out to prospects and how to introduce yourself or your business to build relationships for you and your business.

Why is client outreach so important? LinkedIn has the advantage of providing marketers professional networking with other professionals. LinkedIn is the social media platform for professionals. That makes it a logical place to find contacts and build relationships with like-minded professionals in your industry.

Reaching out via LinkedIn is the key to building your prospect list. But it should be done in a way that doesn't offend or annoy the prospect. And you don't want to reach out to everyone hoping that you connect with the right ones for you.

In this module, you'll discover how to create an effective outreach funnel to build your prospect list. You'll also find out how to build an overall prospect outreach strategy, the right way to message prospects and how to provide value when doing so. And how to tap into the LinkedIn advanced search features to get in front of your prospects.

Overall Strategy

Your outreach strategy should be to provide value to the prospect and to get them to pay attention to you and what you have to offer. But with thousands of others vying for attention it can be difficult.

Use these tips as part of your overall strategy.

1. **Have a complete profile filled out with a professional photo and background image**. Include a professional photo, head, and shoulders only, as it's the first thing people see on your profile. The background image should show your interests, show your connections, create a positive association, or explain what it is you do.

2. **Have an intriguing headline that pulls people into your profile**. It should introduce prospects to your job tile, the business or industry, how you authentically help and what makes working with you special.

3. **Be a thought leader** by sharing one of your research reports to prospective individuals on LinkedIn.

4. **Share targeted relevant data** that only you can share about your industry.

5. **Connect with the employees of potential prospects**. When they see you are connected to others in their organization it can increase your chances of getting the real prospect's attention. Their employees will see your content which they can share with their employer. For example, you share a LinkedIn Publisher post and one of the employees finds value in it and interacts with you. The post ends up in the stream of the employer. You can see all the employees of a company by going to the company page and clicking on "See all employees on LinkedIn."

6. **Consistently publish articles on LinkedIn**, creating and sharing valuable content for your prospects. These articles stay within your profile so new viewers can instantly see them.

7. Try to **post daily status updates**. These can be content you created or curated content, an interesting statistic, or some type of thought-provoking statement.

8. **Like, comment and share other people's updates**, especially your prospects, that are appropriate to your niche.

9. **Follow your potential prospects on LinkedIn and other social platforms**. Interact with them in a natural way on other platforms by liking, commenting, and sharing their posts.

10. Look for ways to **start a conversation with your potential prospect** by commenting or asking a question about their post or update.

11. To stand out from the crowd you need to think creatively. **Do something uncommon that brings value to your prospects**. Create a short one minute (or less) social video with a personalized message after you connect with someone. Address them by name, introduce yourself and compliment them, their company, or their content. Then, thank them for connecting with you.

12. **Become a resource for those in your industry**. By consistently providing value you establish yourself as an authority and will be seen by your potential prospects.

13. **Use visuals to make an impact**. Think about what you want to say then create it with a custom GIF.

14. **Add value immediately and often**. Give in advance before you ask for your prospect's time and attention. Ask yourself what value you can provide them. Provide relevant articles, white papers, or statistics about your industry. Introduce like-minded people to one another, suggest experts that can help them, or any other type of out-of-the-box thinking.

15. **Connect via LinkedIn's InMail messaging feature**. It allows you to send messages you don't have a current connection with on LinkedIn's platform. InMail is a premium feature which means you must subscribe to it but your prospect does not have to be a subscriber.

In this time when everyone is super busy and easily distracted, getting prospects to notice you is difficult. Meeting your prospects with a mindset of offering value to them first is necessary for standing out among the crowd.

6 Killer Methods To Providing Value

While having an overall strategy of providing value is important to being seen, the methods of providing that value might be elusive. If everyone is sharing articles, then how can you stand out?

Here are 6 methods you can use to provide value to your prospects.

1. **Send helpful content to your LinkedIn prospect**. You aren't looking for any personal gain with this information. Instead you are sending it because you know it will be of value to them. The content should specifically benefit the prospect. Tell them why you thought it might interest them.

2. **Be the intermediary**. Connect your LinkedIn connections to each other who would both benefit from it. Many of

these prospects will remember you and think of you when they come across someone has a need for what you offer.

3. Add value by **commenting on other LinkedIn member's updates or content**. Have a clear objective in mind when starting a conversation with prospects. Know the purpose of your comment, how it will add value to the conversation, and will it drive an action or broader conversation.

4. **Offer to do something for your prospects**. For example, if you live in the same area as your prospect, offer to take them out for coffee. Or offer to send them something they can use, perhaps a list of resources for a project they are doing.

5. **Post videos of relevant content that helps your prospects solve a problem**. Don't try to sell yourself or your products during this video – it's information only.

6. **Post created or curated content status updates daily** that is relevant and helpful to your prospects.

Your prospects are looking for ways you can help them with something. By providing value, you are ensuring them you are an authority and helpful.

5 Thing You Must Do To Avoid Annoying Your LinkedIn Prospects

You know how important it is to provide value now, but don't bombard your prospects to the point you are annoying them. You want them to want to reach out to you.

1. Stop inviting people to join your network without sending them a customized invitation of why you want to connect.

2. It's okay to be persistent but for a reasonable length of time. If you don't get a response from your request, wait at least 3-5 days before reaching out again. It's okay to reach out a week or so later if you still haven't gotten a response. Be sure to provide why you've been trying to connect with them and provide one or two relevant items of your content.

3. Not doing your research is a big annoyance to prospects. When reaching out to prospects make it mostly about them and what you can do to benefit them. Know about the person and the company. Find out their pain points.

4. Not giving them time to respond. People are busier than ever. It can be difficult to get through messages and requests. Allow enough time for them to read your pitch and do some research on your business.

5. Not knowing when to give up. Don't keep sending messages after a month, though, since not everyone is interested in working with you.

No one likes a pushy person. Keep these tips in mind when you are reaching out to prospects.

Advanced Search Techniques

You've learned how to reach out to prospects and how not to annoy them. Now you are ready to add new prospects to your list. You can easily find them using LinkedIn's advanced search features. The advanced search allows you to filter your search in different ways.

LinkedIn's Advanced Search allows you to filter by location, industry, past company, current company, connection degree, schools, regions, nonprofit interests, and language. Using the filters allows you to narrow down your filters to prospects that will be the closest fit for your business.

The advanced search lets you save up to three searches. Saved searches is a way to have LinkedIn send you leads based on your already set up search parameters.

Begin by clicking on the search bar in LinkedIn. In the drop-down box, click people.

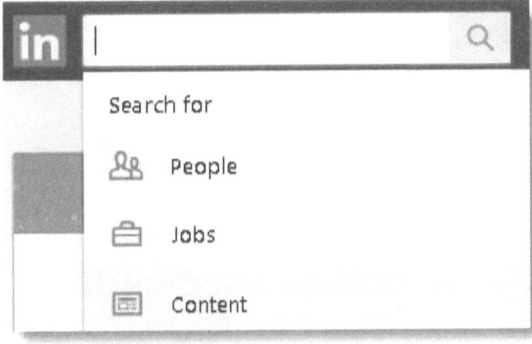

Once on the People search page, click on "All Filters." This brings up the different types of filters you can use to search.

This opens a wide variety of search functions. You should already know your prospect persona with an idea of the job title, their location or target industry. Using that information fill out the sections and then hit apply.

Fill out the connections for any or all of these:
- Location
- Connections of who
- Connection level
- Current company
- Past companies
- Industries
- Profile language
- Schools
- First/Last Name
- Company
- Title

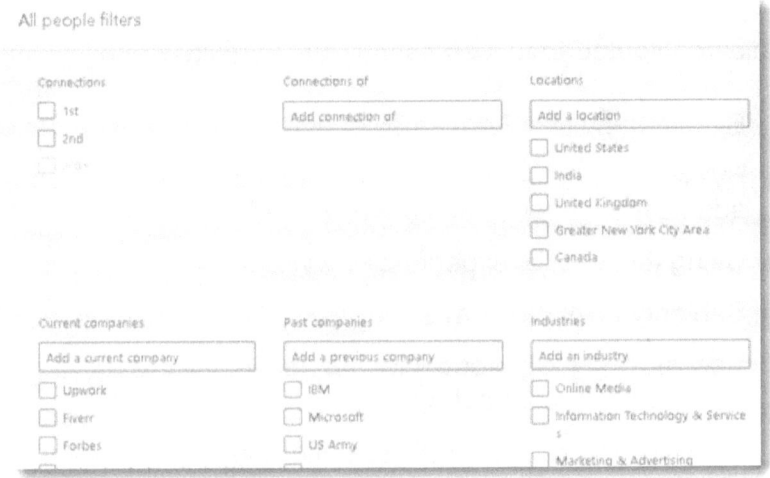

The free LinkedIn version has some restrictions in the advanced search. You're allow a limited number of saved searches per month, limited search filters, and limited to contacting prospects to those you are connected with. InMail is not available on the free version.

If you are looking to dig deeper in your searches, then the paid subscriptions such as LinkedIn Sales Navigator might be the better option.

Why You Need To Use LinkedIn Sales Navigator

LinkedIn sales navigator is a specialized CRM for prospecting. With it you get enhanced search with additional filters. With the Sales Navigator you can save up to 15 different searches.

- Lead suggestions based on your search filters

- Actionable insights to use for when you reach out to leads

- Warm introductions using the TeamLink function.

- InMail allows you to send messages to people you aren't connected to

- Access to LinkedIn insights

The sales navigator advanced search functionality filters include:

- By company size from small business to large corporations
- By what function or role the prospect has in their job: administrative, business development, or marketing.
- Using the level of experience by years
- Seniority level they have
- Specific interest prospects are looking for such as new opportunities, contractors
- Search based on what specific LinkedIn Groups they belong to

The advanced search feature on LinkedIn allows you to dig deeper into finding the prospects that are the best fit for your business.

Your 5 Steps Outreach Funnel

Building a useful prospect list and knowing how to reach out to build relationships is crucial for getting more business. The first step is to find your prospects then you want to begin building an outreach funnel that gets you the appointment.

Step 1: Begin by finding your prospects. This can be done in several ways.

- Go to the profiles of people you are already connected with and look at the sidebar where it lists names of in the People Also Viewed section
- Look at who's viewed your profile
- Look at your competitor's connections
- Connect with people who have endorsed your existing connections

- Do a search using LinkedIn's advanced search feature to find relevant prospects

Step 2: Before approaching a prospect, have a complete profile

- Make sure your summary and profile is up to date
- Have a professional photo and background
- You are sharing useful content
- Share videos, images and SlideShare content on your feed and page that is helpful to your industry
- You are participating in Group conversations.

Step 3: Research prospects.

- Read their summary and view their LinkedIn page
- Look at your current connections. See who they are connected to
- Research your prospects business
- Connect with employees of the business you want to connect to

Step 4: Connect with your prospects

- LinkedIn Articles can be published with a call to action and link to landing page. Distribute them by messaging, share in groups or as sponsored content ads. When your article is published, your connections get notified.

- Sponsored posts LinkedIn allows you sponsor your highest-quality articles. Use LinkedIn's specific targeting criteria to reach prospects. The more likes and shares you get, LinkedIn begin showing your articles in searches and content suggestions.

- SlideShare is considered one of the largest platforms for consumable content sharing. It's good for mobile devices. You can embed SlideShares in your articles. Distribute them by sharing to groups, direct messages, or sponsored ads.

- Webinars is one of the best ways to reach people and engage in your market. You can promote your webinar on LinkedIn by adding links to it to your profile, sending direct messages to connections, sharing to groups and adding links in articles.

- Direct Messages can be used to distribute valuable content, invite prospects to webinars, events, or initiate discovery calls.

- Updates are good for sharing a series of high-value blog posts.

Step 5: Getting the lead or appointment

- Begin reaching out
- Share valuable content with your prospect
- Begin building relationships
    - Send a message thanking them for the connection
    - Share useful blogs and content on your feed
    - Interact with their content
    - Endorse them for skills you witness after you get to know them
- Use LinkedIn InMail to message your prospects
- Keep your message short and personalized
- When you outreach prospects, insert a reference to something in their LinkedIn summary that caught your eye. Or talk about a responsibility they have that makes them a good fit for your offering.

- Send each prospect a personalized invitation to connect
- Craft a compelling first message
- Send new connections a "warm-up" message that includes your free content
- Customize the message based on your research of the prospect and their business
- Use intriguing headlines
- Reply to any leads who engage with you via messages or your content
- Send follow up messages after connecting with them
- Don't try to sell the first time you connect
- Don't annoy the prospect by repeatedly sending messages. Send one message then wait 4 to 7 days before sending another one with valuable content

The outreach funnel is crucial for building a lasting relationship of valuable prospects. From finding the right prospect for your company to researching and reaching out, each step should be done from a place of adding value to their life.

What to Do Next

In this module, you learned the importance of the proper way to reach out to prospects and how to introduce yourself or your business to build relationships for you and your business.

The overall strategy for reaching out to prospects includes creating and sharing valuable content, knowing who your targeted prospects are, having a complete profile and professional photo. Your profile is the first thing prospects see so it should be compelling, intriguing, humorous or some other emotion that says who you are.

You should be providing value to your prospects in the form of articles, feed updates, blog posts, videos, images or SlideShare presentations. The content can be what you have created or curated content from within your industry.

When reaching out to prospects you want to avoid annoying them. After they have responded to you in some way, invite them to connect. Then send them messages or emails with valuable content occasionally.

Once you have exhausted your source for first- and second-degree prospects, you can do a LinkedIn advanced search to find more targeted leads. The search allows you to use specific parameters to find prospects.

Finally having an outreach funnel allows you to know exactly which steps to take next in building your prospect list and connecting with them.

DOWNLOAD YOUR MODULE FOUR RESOURCES:

Download the following resources for this module at https://Linkedin.Leads-Machines.com/registration-bonus-membership

RESOURCE ONE
Detailed checklist (2 pages) to keep you on track as you start building relationships you're your prospects.

RESOURCE TWO
Detailed worksheet (3 pages) to help you as you begin reaching out and building relationships.

Conclusion

In the 4 modules in this book, you have learned the P.A.C.E approach:

1. **Profile** - How to set up your profile with important settings and optimization strategies.

2. **Attract** - How to optimize your LinkedIn Company page and profile to attract your leads in.

3. **Content -** How to dominate with content on LinkedIn.

4. **Extract** - How to create a client outreach plan and extract out maximum prospect list

Now it's time to put it into action and build up your LinkedIn Leads Machines in the next 45 days. Go for it!

To Your Success,
-- Keith Choy

FREE BONUS Resources

DOWNLOAD YOUR BONUS RESOURCES:

The following resources are available in our Bonus Online Resource Area at https://Linkedin.Leads-Machines.com/registration-bonus-membership

BONUS ONE
Checklists and Worksheets
All the 6 checklists/worksheets from our 4 modules so that you can print them out and fill in your details directly. This will save you effort and time.

BONUS TWO
Infographic on Getting New Leads
Infographic summarizing all the key steps you need to take. It is a good reference map which you will keep going back to.

BONUS THREE
LinkedIn Messaging Templates
These templates will help you optimize and build relationships with LinkedIn. No more writers' block. It includes:

- 2 Message Templates which you can personalize and use to get you started on getting recommendations on LinkedIn.
- 10 LinkedIn Prospect Messaging Templates to begin connecting with your LinkedIn prospects.
- 20 LinkedIn Headline Templates to help you come up with a killer headline. Your LinkedIn headline is one of the most visible areas on your profile. You want it to be intriguing, compelling, and interesting enough to get your prospects attention.

BONUS FOUR
Relationship Building Tactics

Building relationships is key to getting leads to become customers. Use this list of 44 tactics as a guide.

BONUS FIVE
Strategies for LinkedIn Optimization Services mini-guide

As you already know, having a complete and fully optimized LinkedIn profile for any business is key to being seen among the millions on the social media platform. Many businesses just don't have the time or want to learn how to optimize their profile and Company pages. That's where your services come in. This mini-guide gives you a starting point on offering this much needed service.

Register For The VIP Members Workshop

Thanks for buying my book. For being my VIP members, I am happy to invite you to VIP Members Workshop.

Please register for this ONE-OFF VIP members only workshop where you will be shown how to generate more than seven figures per year with free traffic!

Go to the link below and select the best time that works for you to attend this webinar!

How To Start A Wildly Profitable 7 Figure Marketing Business & Start Earning Commissions TONIGHT

http://Leads-Machines.com/go/vip-members-workshop.htm

Check Out Other Books In Leads-Machines Series

www.Leads-Machines.com

LinkedIn Leads Machines

LinkedIn.Leads-Machines.com

Pinterest Leads Machines

Pinterest.Leads-Machines.com

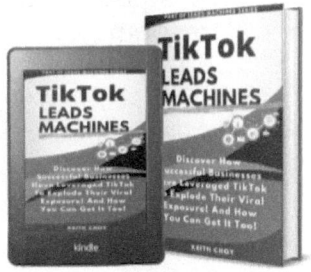

TikTok Leads Machines

TikTok.Leads-Machines.com

ABOUT THE AUTHOR

Keith Choy started his paths to leave the rat race over 19 years ago with zero experiences after being inspired by Robert Allen and Tony Robbins in Singapore. Since then, he has ventured into Stock Trading, Options Trading, Internet Marketing, Infoprenuer and Property investments with various levels of success. Through his journeys, he has also learnt from his failures and improve the process. His personal mission is to spread his experiences and help others start their path to achieve financial freedom.

www.ingramcontent.com/pod-product-compliance
Lightning Source LLC
Chambersburg PA
CBHW021456210526
45463CB00002B/794